ANIMAL LIVES

SNAKES & REPTILES

STICKER ACTIVITY BOOK

by Sally Morgan

Silver Dolphin

San Diego, California

Silver Dolphin Books
An imprint of the
Advantage Publishers Group
10350 Barnes Canyon Road
San Diego, CA 92121
www.silverdolphinbooks.com

ISBN-13: 978-1-59223-920-7
ISBN-10: 1-59223-920-X

Made in China.

Created by Walter Foster Publishing, Inc.
Creative Direction by Pauline Foster
Concept development by Pauline Foster
and Heidi Kellenberger
Guidebook written by Sally Morgan
Activity cards written by Sandy Phan
Art Direction by David Rosemeyer
and Shelley Baugh
Production Design by Debbie Aiken
Production Management by Nicole
Szawlowski, Irene Chan, and
Rushi Sanathra

1   2   3   4   5   12   11   10   09   08

Molting

A snake's scaly skin is tough and does not stretch. As a snake grows, its skin gets tight. Young snakes must **molt,** or shed their skins, to grow bigger.

When snakes are ready to molt, an oil spreads under the outer layer of skin. The old skin splits and slips off in one piece, leaving shiny new skin underneath.

Snakes never stop growing. They molt whenever they grow too big for their skin.

SNAKE FACT

Snakes do not have eyelids to protect their eyes. Instead they have a see-through scale covering each eye.

Slithering

Snakes do not have legs like lizards and other reptiles. They move in a completely different way—they slither along the ground.

The body of this rattlesnake forms a series of curves as it winds across the ground.

Tree snakes, such as this boomslang, have long, thin bodies. They spread their weight across many branches.

Wiggling and gliding

Most snakes wiggle across the ground, moving from side to side. The snake's body follows its head in a series of curves. Heavy snakes and those that creep up on their **prey** glide slowly forward in a straight line. The scales underneath their body hook onto the ground, pulling the snake forward.

Sidewinding

It is difficult for a snake to slither across sand because it is too loose to push against. Snakes that live in deserts, such as sidewinders, have found the answer—they move sideways.

Sidewinders throw their head sideways while the rest of their body stays on the ground. Once their head is back on the ground, the rest of the body follows the head sideways, creating a curling movement.

SNAKE FACT

Snakes cannot slither very quickly. Even the fastest-moving snakes, the African mambas, travel at only 9 miles per hour over a short distance.

The tracks of the sidewinder show that not all of its body touches the ground at the same time.

Turn to page 103 to find the sticker that completes this scene.

Snake senses

Snakes use their senses to find their way around and to catch prey. Snakes cannot see very well, but they have excellent hearing and a very good sense of smell. Their ears are completely covered but can pick up **vibrations** in the ground. These vibrations tell them if an animal is moving nearby.

Snakes flick out their forked tongue through a slot in their upper jaw.

Forked tongues

Snakes taste the air with their forked tongue. When a snake flicks its tongue out of its mouth, the tongue picks up scent particles from the air. The tongue's forks are then pushed into a special sense organ on the roof of the snake's mouth.

Hunting at night

Pit vipers and pythons hunt at night. They cannot see much in the dark, but they can detect the heat given off by the bodies of their prey. Snakes do this using heat-sensitive pits on their face.

Pit vipers can detect heat with the pits on their snout.

SNAKE FACT

Blind snakes do not have any eyes at all. This is not a problem because they live in dark caves and rely on their other senses to find their way around.

QUESTION

What process do snakes go through in order to grow?

Find the sticker on page 105 that represents the correct answer.

Answer: Molting, or shedding their skin (see page 15)

Create a scene

Use the stickers on page 97
to create your own snake habitat!

20

21

Predators

Snakes are **predators,** which means they kill other animals for food. Many snakes hunt a range of animals, from insects and worms to lizards and mice. Others hunt only one kind of animal. For example, hook-nosed snakes eat only spiders.

It is not just small animals that get eaten by snakes. Big animals, like deer, goats, and even people, get swallowed up by snakes like giant boa constrictors and pythons.

The Gabon viper's color and pattern helps it hide among fallen leaves while it waits to ambush prey.

Swallowing prey

Snakes do not have any feet, so they cannot hold their food and bite chunks out of it. Instead, snakes swallow their prey in one piece, usually headfirst.

Snakes can open their mouth very wide, because their lower jaw is loosely joined to the bottom of their skull. This means even large animals can fit through.

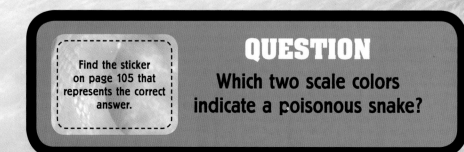

Find the sticker on page 105 that represents the correct answer.

QUESTION

Which two scale colors indicate a poisonous snake?

22

Answer: Red and yellow (see page 9)

Snakes have backward-facing teeth to keep their prey from escaping.

SNAKE FACT

The common egg-eater snake swallows bird eggs that are up to four times the size of its head. That's like a person swallowing a car tire.

23

Constrictors

Many of the largest snakes, such as the boas and pythons, are constrictors. These snakes squeeze, or constrict, their prey to death.

Tighter and tighter

Once a constrictor has trapped its prey, it coils its body around the victim. The coils get tighter and tighter. As the prey breathes out, the snake tightens the coils. Eventually the victim cannot breathe or pump blood around its body.

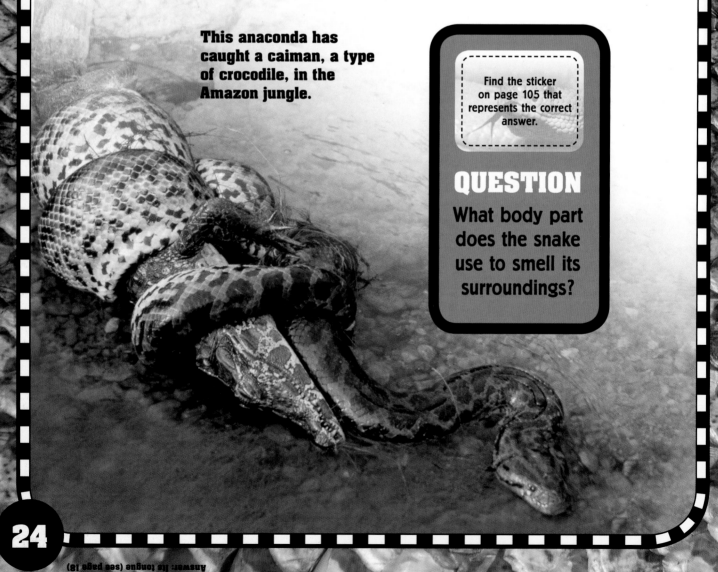

This anaconda has caught a caiman, a type of crocodile, in the Amazon jungle.

Find the sticker on page 105 that represents the correct answer.

QUESTION

What body part does the snake use to smell its surroundings?

Answer: Its tongue (see page 18)

Swallowed whole

Once the prey is dead, the snake relaxes and uncoils slightly, and begins to swallow its victim headfirst.

The snake's skin is very elastic and it stretches to make room for a large meal. This makes a bulge in the snake's body, which gradually moves along the body, getting smaller as it is digested. Many snakes do not eat regular meals. The largest snakes can survive on one good meal a year.

The constrictor wraps itself around its prey so the animal cannot escape.

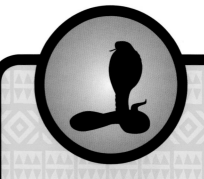

SNAKE FACT

The world's largest snake, the green anaconda of South America, is powerful enough to kill caimans. This giant snake ambushes its prey in the water.

Poisonous snakes

Many snakes produce **venom**. They do this to kill their prey and to protect themselves if they are threatened.

The most poisonous snakes are the vipers, cobras, sea snakes, and the Australian brown snakes. They use their venom to kill prey and fight off attackers.

Spitting cobras spit venom into the eyes of their prey to blind them.

SNAKE FACT

One of the most poisonous snakes is the Australian inland taipan. The venom in one bite is enough to kill 200,000 mice!

Find the sticker on page 105 that represents the correct answer.

QUESTION

How do boas and pythons kill their prey?

Answer: They constrict their prey (see page 24)

Fangs

A snake's venom is produced in a gland in its head and is pumped into its prey through a long, sharp tooth, called a fang. When the snake bites, the venom flows along the fang into the prey. Some venom kills quickly, while other venom just weakens the prey.

Some venom may start to break down the skin around the bite. The venom of the western diamondback rattlesnake does this.

This sedge viper is ready to attack. Its fangs are on its upper jaw.

The red, yellow, and black stripes of this coral snake warn other animals that it is very poisonous.

27

Snake defenses

Snakes may be predators, but they are often hunted by other animals; for example, mongooses and secretary birds are expert snake killers. They can even kill a snake that has deadly venom.

Camouflage

Venomous snakes can fight back when attacked, but nonpoisonous snakes have other ways of protecting themselves. Most snakes are well **camouflaged** and they lie still so predators cannot spot them easily.

The mongoose attacks and kills poisonous snakes, such as this cobra.

Turn to page 103 to find the sticker that completes this scene.

SNAKE FACT

The rubber boa's head and tail are difficult to tell apart. When threatened, the snake rolls into a ball and waves its tail, pretending its tail is its head.

Copy cats

Several nonvenomous snakes pretend to be poisonous by looking similar to a venomous species. The bright colors scare off a predator, who thinks it might get bitten.

The harmless milk snake is often mistaken for the poisonous coral snake.

Turn to page 103 to find the sticker that completes this scene.

When threatened, the grass snake pretends to be dead.

Snakes and people

Many people are scared of snakes even though most snakes are harmless. People think that snakes are cold, slimy animals, but they are warm and dry to the touch.

Death from snakebites

Only a few snakes will attack a person; most will just slither away. But if the snake feels threatened, it will strike. In places where there are many dangerous snakes, such as India, people often get bitten. There are medicines that stop the venom from working. However, if a person who has been bitten does not get treatment quickly, he or she may die.

A rattlesnake has a rattle on its tail, which is used to scare away attackers. The rattle is made up of sections of dried skin that knock together.

SNAKE FACT

As many as 100,000 people die each year from snakebites, mostly in remote areas of Africa and India.

Find the sticker on page 105 that represents the correct answer.

QUESTION

Q: What do grass snakes do when threatened?

Useful venom

Scientists are using some snake venom to make medicines; for example, one venom is used to reduce high blood pressure. The venom is removed from the snake in a process called **milking**.

31

Answer: Play dead (see page 29)

Snakes under threat

Many snakes are under threat, and some species may even become **extinct**.

Habitat loss

The main reason why many snakes are dying out is because their **habitats** are being destroyed. The forests and meadows where snakes live are being turned into farms and towns.

Snakes that live in tropical rain forests cannot survive anywhere else once the forest is cleared.

Hunted

Snakes are often killed because they are poisonous. For example, rattlesnakes are sometimes killed in huge numbers in the United States. Other snakes are killed for their skins, which are used to make handbags, shoes, and souvenirs. The beautiful but deadly sea krait is especially rare because of this.

Snakeskin is soft and the scales make an attractive pattern.

Conserving snakes

It is very important that habitats are saved to protect endangered snakes. Many species that are under threat of extinction are bred in zoos. They may be released into the wild in the future.

Thousands of sea kraits are caught each year for their skin.

Life cycle

The female snake lays a clutch of eggs on the ground. Tiny snakes that look like miniature adults hatch after one to three months. The young snakes grow quickly and shed their skin regularly. Most snakes live for about 10 years, but some live as long as 40 years in zoos.

Baby snake hatching out of an egg

Fully grown snake

Molting

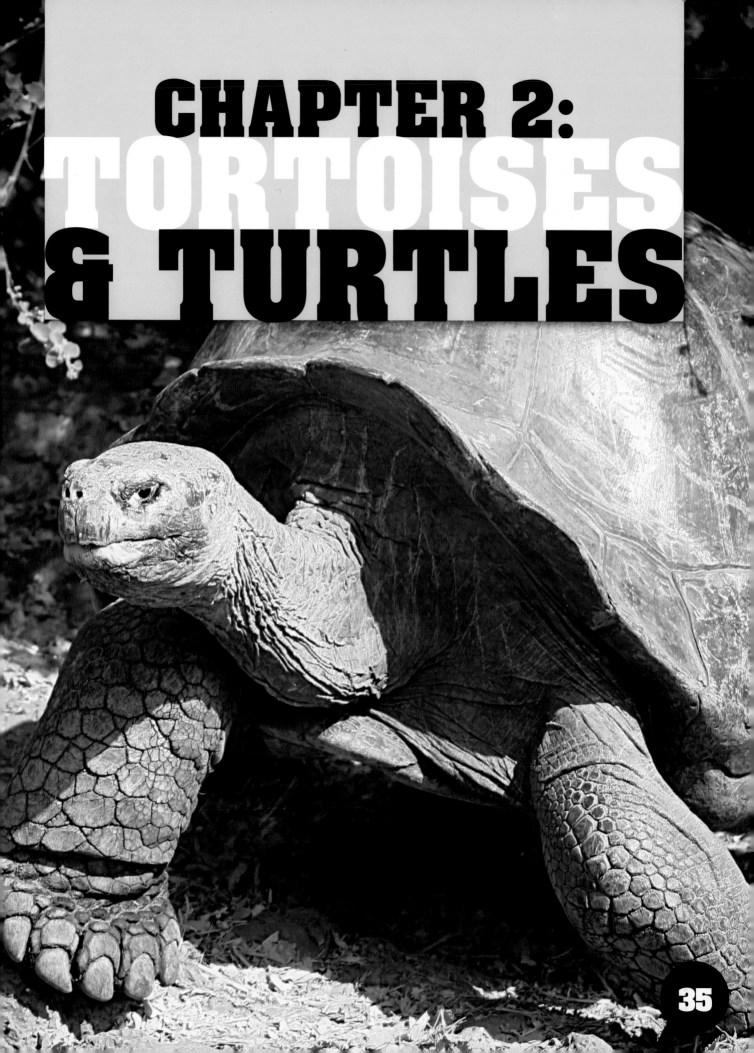

CHAPTER 2:
TORTOISES
& TURTLES

TORTOISES & TURTLES

Tortoises and turtles are **ancient** animals that first appeared on earth more than 200 million years ago, when the dinosaurs were alive. Their appearance has changed very little in all this time. They are easy to recognize because they have a heavy shell covering their back.

TURTLE FACT

The largest turtle is the giant leatherback. Its shell can be up to 8 feet long and can weigh more than 1,900 pounds.

This Cagle's map turtle has a flatter shell than a tortoise.

This giant tortoise has a heavy, domed shell and thick legs.

Turn to page 103 to find the sticker that completes this scene.

Reptiles

Turtles and tortoises are related to lizards, snakes, and crocodiles. They belong to a group of animals called reptiles, which have scaly skin and lay leathery eggs.

Tortoises are land animals but turtles spend most of their life either in or by water. Freshwater turtles are found in rivers, lakes, and swamps, while sea turtles are found in the oceans. Some freshwater turtles are called **terrapins,** which means "little turtle."

Types of tortoises and turtles

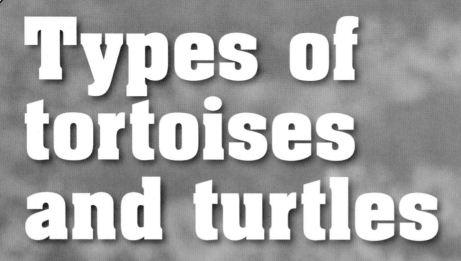

Some turtles and tortoises, such as this snapping turtle, have extra armor on their shells.

There are about 290 species, or types, of tortoises and turtles, and all of them have a shell. There are a total of 60 bones in the shell, which is covered by large scales for extra protection. Turtles have a flattish shell, which is a better shape for swimming. Tortoises, however, have a domed shell, which gives them more protection from predators.

Hiding in shells

Tortoises and turtles can be divided into two groups: the hidden-necked and the side-necked. Hidden-necked turtles and tortoises pull their heads directly inside their shells by forming an S-shaped curve with their necks. Side-necked turtles pull their heads under the edge of their shells by bending their necks sideways.

Tortoises pull their heads into their shells to protect themselves from predators.

Find the sticker on page 105 that represents the correct answer.

QUESTION

What is the name of the largest turtle, whose shell can grow up to 8 feet long and can weigh more than 1,900 pounds?

Where do tortoises and turtles live?

All over the world

Turtles and tortoises are found on every continent except Antarctica. Tortoises and freshwater turtles are found mainly in **tropical** and subtropical climates. The greatest variety of freshwater turtles is found in India and Bangladesh, and in the southern United States. Tortoises are also found in southern Europe.

Find the sticker on page 105 that represents the correct answer.

QUESTION

What is the word used to describe some small freshwater turtles?

Answer: Terrapin (see page 37)

NORTH AMERICA

EUROPE

ASIA

ATLANTIC OCEAN

AFRICA

PACIFIC OCEAN

PACIFIC OCEAN

SOUTH AMERICA

INDIAN OCEAN

AUSTRALIA

Areas where turtles are found

Areas where tortoises are found

SOUTHERN OCEAN

ANTARCTICA

Leopard tortoises are found in Africa. They live in woodland areas and on the grasslands.

Ocean living

Sea turtles are found mostly in tropical oceans, but some species swim far north, almost to the Arctic. They can be found in the deep ocean, too. Turtles do not have to come to the surface to breathe because they can take in oxygen from the water through their skin and throat. This means they can stay underwater for weeks at a time.

Beginning life

The female tortoise digs a hole in which she lays her eggs, and then she covers them.

Turtles and tortoises lay leathery eggs. The female tortoise or turtle lays between one and 240 eggs at a time, depending on her species. The time taken for the eggs to hatch also varies, from two months to more than a year.

Nesting on beaches

Female sea turtles return to the beach where they were born to lay their eggs. At night, they haul themselves up onto the beach and dig a deep hole in the sand in which to lay their eggs. The eggs hatch a few months later and the **hatchlings** dig their way to the surface. Most hatchlings emerge at night, when they are less likely to be seen by predators, and make a quick dash to the sea. Some sea turtles lay several clutches of eggs each year.

Find the sticker on page 105 that represents the correct answer.

QUESTION

On which continent are there no turtles or tortoises?

These hatchlings have made it to the safety of the water.

Answer: Antarctica (see page 41)

Growing up

It takes these desert tortoises five years to grow to a length of just 3 inches.

Hatchlings look like miniature adults. They range in size from just 1 inch to about 3 inches long. They are on their own from the moment they hatch because their parents do not look after them. Many young tortoises and turtles die during their first few years. A lot are eaten by predators and others die due to a lack of food. Young tortoises living in dry habitats may also die during droughts.

Turn to page 103 to find the stickers that complete this scene.

Growth

Young tortoises and turtles grow rapidly during their first few years, and then growth slows down. The smaller species stop growing when their shell reaches about 5 inches long. The larger species continue to grow throughout their lives.

Long lives

Once they are adults, the number of tortoises and turtles that die is very small. In fact, they have one of the longest life spans of any animal. Tortoises and turtles in captivity live to be about 70 years of age. In the wild, they live for 30 to 40 years. Some, however, live considerably longer. Box turtles, for example, can live for 100 years.

TORTOISE FACT

The oldest known animal in the world was a Galápagos giant tortoise called Harriet. She lived to be 175 years old, and died in 2006.

Scientists can identify the age of some turtles from growth marks on their scales.

Getting around

Turtles and tortoises move around in different ways. Tortoises are well known for walking very slowly, but turtles can swim surprisingly quickly.

On land

Tortoises are adapted to moving on land. They have large feet with short toes. To walk, they raise their heavy bodies off the ground. Their walking speed is just 0.3 to 0.5 miles per hour.

Tortoises need sturdy legs to lift their heavy bodies off the ground.

In the water

Freshwater turtles have to be able to walk on land and swim in water. Many of these turtles live in shallow water and walk over the bottoms of lakes or rivers. When they swim, they tend to use all four legs as paddles.

Snake-necked turtles are found in Australia, where they live both on land and in water.

Turn to page 103 to find the sticker that completes this scene.

Sea turtles use their flippers to push themselves through the water.

At sea

Sea turtles spend their lives in the ocean and are powerful and graceful swimmers. Their shell has a flat shape that slips easily through the water. They have long toes that are joined together to form flipperlike paddles. They use their hind legs as a rudder for steering.

Tortoise and turtle senses

Tortoises and turtles have senses that enable them to find their way around and to find food. The senses of a turtle are slightly different from those of a tortoise because they live in water.

Color vision helps this green turtle find food on coral reefs.

Smell

Turtles have an excellent sense of smell and this enables them to find food. They "smell" the water by opening their mouths slightly, drawing the water in through their noses, and pushing it out through their mouths.

European pond turtles live in murky water, so they rely on their sense of smell and hearing to catch their prey.

Find the sticker on page 105 that represents the correct answer.

QUESTION

What are newly hatched baby turtles called?

Sight

Both tortoises and turtles have good eyesight and can see in color. Sight is important for finding food, and turtles and tortoises are particularly attracted to foods that are green, red, and yellow. Turtles' eyes have adapted so that they can see underwater, too.

Hearing

Tortoises can hear sounds, while turtles can feel vibrations in the water. This tells them where food—or a predator—might be.

Touch

Turtles and tortoises have a network of nerves that run over the surface of their shells. This means they can sense anything that touches them.

Create a scene

Use the stickers on page 99
to create your own turtle habitat!

Feeding

Adult green turtles are unusual because they feed only on plants such as algae and sea grass.

Tortoises and turtles do not have any teeth. Instead, they have a beaklike structure around their strong jaws. Tortoises eat mostly leaves, fruit, and slow-moving animals such as snails and worms. Sea turtles eat a variety of animal foods, including jellyfish, corals, sea urchins, crabs, and fish.

TURTLE FACT

The matamata, a type of freshwater turtle, lies in wait for a fish to come by. Then it opens its mouth wide and expands its throat, sucking the fish straight into its mouth!

Hunting

Tortoises and most freshwater turtles move too slowly to hunt prey. Some get around this problem by lying in wait for prey animals to pass by. One of the most aggressive turtles is the snapping turtle, which eats almost anything as long as it can catch and swallow it.

Find the sticker on page 105 that represents the correct answer.

QUESTION

What do sea turtles use to help push themselves through the water?

Sea turtles, such as this hawksbill, feed on jellyfish that float in the water.

Predators

Predators such as crabs gather on the beach to catch and eat the hatchling turtles.

Tortoises and turtles have many different predators. Their eggs are dug up and eaten by animals such as monitor lizards and raccoons, and hatchlings are eaten by birds and other animals.

As they get larger, turtles and tortoises are less likely to be attacked by other animals. Their shell patterns and colors give them camouflage, so it can be difficult to spot them. The domed shell of tortoises also makes it hard for a predator to grip the animal in its jaws.

QUESTION

True or false? Tortoises and turtles do not have any teeth.

Hunted

Humans are predators of turtles, too. In many parts of the world, people eat turtle meat and eggs. Some countries have banned this, but the hunting still goes on.

In places such as El Salvador, Guatemala, and Mexico, sea turtle eggs are dug up and sold as delicacies.

Answer: True (see page 52)

Ectothermic

Tortoises and turtles are ectothermic, or cold-blooded, animals. This means that their body temperature changes with the temperature of their surroundings. Ectothermic animals are active only when they are warm. In the morning, tortoises and freshwater turtles can be seen basking in the sun to warm up.

TORTOISE FACT

The Horsfield's tortoise, which lives in Kazakhstan (central Asia), stays underground for nine months of the year. It emerges only when it rains and there is vegetation available for it to eat.

Hibernation

Tortoises and freshwater turtles that live in cooler temperate regions cannot survive the cold winter months. The temperatures are too cold for them to be active, and there is no food. To survive, they go into a type of deep sleep called **hibernation**. Tortoises sleep in burrows in the ground. Freshwater turtles hibernate in mud at the bottom of pools. They survive by absorbing oxygen from the water through their skin.

Eastern box turtles emerge from hibernation in April, when the weather is warmer.

These painted turtles have climbed onto a log so that they can sit in the sun and warm their bodies.

Turn to page 103 to find the sticker that completes this scene.

Migrating turtles

Most freshwater turtles feed and nest in the same area. However, sea turtles make a long journey every year or so to return to the beaches where they were born and lay their eggs. This regular journey is called a **migration.**

Hundreds of female turtles have arrived at the same time to lay their eggs on this beach in Costa Rica.

Turtles, such as this hawksbill, navigate their way across huge oceans.

Finding their way

Scientists are unsure how the turtles manage to find their way across the oceans. It may involve smelling the water, or even using a sense that scientists do not yet know about.

Find the sticker on page 105 that represents the correct answer.

QUESTION

True or false? Tortoises and freshwater turtles like to bask in the sun to warm themselves in the morning.

Answer: True (see page 56)

Living alone

Most tortoises and turtles live a **solitary** life, coming into contact with others only when they feed in the same area or when they mate. Tortoises usually live in a particular area, called a territory. However, unlike many other animals that have territories, they do not defend their territory from other tortoises. Thus, the territories of different tortoises may overlap.

TURTLE FACT

Some turtles, such as roofed turtles and South American river turtles, clean each other. One turtle uses its jaws to pull algae off the other, and then they switch places.

The Texas tortoise lives alone in dry, sandy areas of Texas and Mexico.

Turn to page 103 to find the sticker that completes this scene.

Tortoises that can stretch their necks the most are more important within the group.

Reaching taller

There are a few species of tortoises that live in groups all the time, such as the giant tortoises of the Galápagos Islands. They have a hierarchy in which some individuals are more important than others. This is based on how high the tortoise can extend its head. A tortoise that can extend its head higher can reach more plants to eat, which means it grows larger.

Tortoises and turtles under threat

Half of all the species of turtles and tortoises are at risk of becoming extinct. Tortoises have suffered from a loss of habitat and from being caught in the wild to be kept as pets. Sea turtles have had their breeding beaches disturbed by tourism and are also caught and eaten in many parts of Asia. Their eggs are also eaten. The shells of tortoises and turtles have been used to make jewelry, and the skin of the Olive Ridley turtle is used as an expensive leather.

Find the sticker on page 105 that represents the correct answer.

QUESTION

What is the word used to describe the journey that freshwater turtles make every year to lay their eggs?

Some sea turtles get caught up in fishing nets.

Answer: Migration (see page 58)

In some places, eggs are moved to conservation centers. When they have hatched, the hatchlings are released back into the water.

Conserving tortoises and turtles

Fortunately, people are trying to look after the remaining tortoises and turtles. Laws have been passed that make it illegal to keep tortoises as pets. The habitats and breeding beaches of tortoises and turtles are also being protected by turning them into nature reserves.

Life cycle

A female turtle is ready to breed when she is between five and 25 years old, depending on the species. She lays a clutch of eggs in the sand. A few months later, the hatchlings break out of the eggs. The young turtles gradually get larger. Turtles live for 30 to 60 years, but some species live even longer.

Egg hatchling

Full-grown turtle

Juvenile

CHAPTER 3: ALLIGATORS & CROCODILES

ALLIGATORS
& CROCODILES

This Australian freshwater crocodile has extra-large scales along its back.

Alligators and crocodiles are fierce predators that live near water and are the largest of the world's reptiles. Reptiles are animals that have skin that is covered with dry scales. Most reptiles, including alligators and crocodiles, lay eggs that have leathery shells. Other reptiles include snakes, turtles, and lizards.

Appearance

Alligators and crocodiles look very similar. They both have long bodies and tails that are covered in thick scales, and legs that stick out to the sides. Most alligators and crocodiles are between 6 and 10 feet long, with the males being much larger than the females.

CROCODILE FACT

The extinct crocodile *Sarcosuchus imperator*, which lived during the time of the dinosaurs, may have reached up to 40 feet long.

Both crocodiles and alligators, such as this American alligator, have a long snout with powerful jaws.

Types of crocodiles and alligators

Gharials use their long, thin snouts to catch fish.

There are 23 different species, or types, of alligators and crocodiles. They are divided into three families: alligators, crocodiles, and gharials.

The alligator family includes caimans and alligators, which range in size from 3 to 13 feet long. The crocodile family includes saltwater, Nile, New Guinea, and American crocodiles. The gharial family includes just the gharial, which has a very long snout with a potlike tip.

Telling the difference

The large fourth tooth in the lower jaw of an alligator fits into a socket in the upper jaw and is not visible when the alligator's mouth is closed. In crocodiles, this tooth is visible even when the crocodile's mouth is shut.

Caimans are small and squat, with extremely toothy grins.

ALLIGATOR FACT

Alligators have between 74 and 80 teeth. As the teeth wear down, they are replaced. An alligator can go through 2,000 to 3,000 teeth in a lifetime.

Where do crocodiles and alligators live?

Alligators and crocodiles are found mostly in the tropical and subtropical parts of the world.

Alligators are found only in the southeastern United States and in China, while caimans are found mostly in Central and South America. Crocodiles are found in many more places, including Florida, Central and South America, Africa, Pakistan, India, Southeast Asia, and northern Australia. The gharial is found in India, Nepal, Burma, and Pakistan.

Find the sticker on page 105 that represents the correct answer.

QUESTION
How many feet long are alligators and crocodiles?

Alligators and crocodiles often spend the day lying in water to keep cool.

Answer: Between 6 and 10 feet (see page 67)

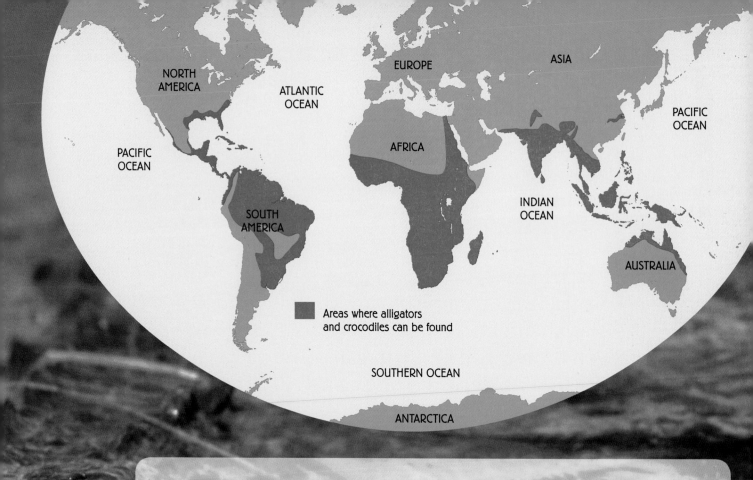

NORTH AMERICA

ATLANTIC OCEAN

EUROPE

ASIA

PACIFIC OCEAN

PACIFIC OCEAN

AFRICA

INDIAN OCEAN

SOUTH AMERICA

AUSTRALIA

■ Areas where alligators and crocodiles can be found

SOUTHERN OCEAN

ANTARCTICA

Wetland habitats

Alligators and crocodiles live in wetland habitats such as tropical rain forests, swamps, along rivers, in coastal **mangroves,** and around ocean islands.

Although alligators and crocodiles can be found in the same areas, they do not live closely together. For example, in the Florida Everglades, the American crocodile is found near the ocean, where the water is partly salty, while alligators are found farther inland, where the water is fresh.

CROCODILE FACT

Saltwater crocodiles can swim long distances. Some have been found on remote islands in the Pacific, more than 800 miles from other crocodiles.

Beginning life

Female alligators and crocodiles lay between 10 and 50 leathery eggs in a nest. Some species dig out a nest in the ground, but others make a mound by using their feet to gather up dirt. Then they lay their eggs inside the mound. By laying her eggs either in the ground or in a mound of dirt, the female makes sure the eggs stay warm.

This Nile crocodile is laying her eggs in a hole in the ground.

ALLIGATOR AND CROCODILE FACT

If the temperature in the nest stays between 89°F and 91°F, most of the hatchlings will be male. If it is below 88°F or above 95°F, most are female.

Guarding the nest

Most reptiles abandon their eggs once they have laid them, but female alligators and crocodiles guard their nests and attack any animal that comes too close. They only leave their nests to cool off in the shade or to go for a quick dip in the water. In some species, the males stay close by, too.

Despite the protection, not all the eggs hatch. Predators, such as monitor lizards and bears, raid the nests. Some nests are lost due to flooding, while others get too hot. Disease also kills some baby alligators or crocodiles before they hatch.

These Nile crocodiles are guarding their eggs.

Turn to page 103 to find the sticker that completes this scene.

Hatching out

The eggs remain in the nest for between two and three months, depending on the species of alligator or crocodile. Just before hatching, the young alligators or crocodiles inside the eggs make lots of high-pitched sounds. These sounds tell the mother that they are about to hatch. She uses her legs to dig up the nest and help her hatchlings get to the surface. Often, she pushes her snout into the nest to find the eggs.

Find the sticker on page 105 that represents the correct answer.

QUESTION

In what types of climates are most alligators and crocodiles found throughout the world?

Hatchlings break out of their eggs by using a special egg tooth at the end of their jaw.

Answer: Tropical and subtropical (see page 70)

CROCODILE FACT

If baby crocodiles are in danger, the mother flips them into her mouth for protection.

When a hatchling can't break out of its egg, the mother takes it in her mouth and gently rolls it backward and forward on her tongue. This opens the shell and allows the hatchling to break free.

Once they have hatched, the mother picks up the hatchlings and carries them to water.

Growing up

The hatchlings stay together after they have hatched. During the day, they spread out to look for food, such as insects and small fish. Their mother is always nearby and she listens for their sounds.

The hatchlings stay with their mother for several months. Young American alligators stay close to their mother for up to two years. When they leave their mother, the young adults move out into the surrounding area.

CROCODILE FACT

Only about 1 percent of young Australian saltwater crocodiles survive to reach adulthood.

Out of every 35 American alligator hatchlings, only six will survive the first year.

Find the sticker on page 105 that represents the correct answer.

QUESTION
How many eggs do female alligators and crocodiles lay in a nest?

Answer: Between 10 and 50 (see page 72)

During their early years, young alligators are tempting prey to larger predators.

Larger is safer

Although young alligators and crocodiles are protected by their mothers, many are killed by predators such as snakes, lizards, birds of prey, hyenas, and tigers; however, the number of alligators and crocodiles killed falls as they get larger. Once they reach a length of 3 feet, they are reasonably safe from predators.

Getting around

Alligators and crocodiles can move on land and in water. On land, they either walk slowly, dragging their tails along the ground, or they raise their bodies and tails up off the ground and walk on their toes. Using this "high walk," they can also gallop surprisingly quickly, but only in a straight line and over a short distance because they soon get tired.

Galloping crocodiles can reach speeds of up to 10 miles per hour.

Find the sticker on page 105 that represents the correct answer.

QUESTION
True or false?
When a hatchling can't break free from its egg, the mother gently rolls it in her mouth to help break the shell.

Answer: True (see page 75)

Crocodiles steer and brake by sticking out their legs.

Swimming

Alligators and crocodiles use their long, muscular tails to propel their bodies through the water. When they swim, they hold their legs close to the sides of their body to create a streamlined shape that glides through the water.

Underwater

Both alligators and crocodiles can float in the water with just their eyes and nostrils above the water. They have a flap that closes off their mouths so they can breathe through their noses. They can dive and stay underwater for several minutes. Some have been known to stay underwater for as long as five hours.

Create a scene

Use the stickers on page 101
to create your own alligator habitat!

Senses

Alligators and crocodiles have excellent senses that they use to find their prey. They have a special sense that enables them to detect movement in the water. Tiny **sensors** scattered over their face, especially around their mouth, can detect the tiniest vibrations caused by animals moving in and around the water.

These strange glowing lights on the surface of the water are reflections from the eyes of alligators.

CROCODILE FACT

Crocodiles have an extra reflective layer at the back of their eye so they can see more at night.

Crocodile eyes

The eyes of these animals are covered by three eyelids. The third eyelid is **transparent** and covers the eye to protect it in the water. Alligators and crocodiles have vertical **pupils** like those of cats, which get larger so they can see more in the dark. However, they cannot see much underwater.

Light passes through the black pupil into the eye of the crocodile.

Find the sticker on page 105 that represents the correct answer.

QUESTION

Out of every 35 American alligator hatchlings, how many will survive the first year?

Answer: Six (see page 76)

Hunting

Alligators and crocodiles feed on a wide range of animals. Most lie in wait for their prey to pass close by. Some alligators and crocodiles float in the water, while others hide in the vegetation at the water's edge.

Powerful jaws

Alligators and crocodiles grab their prey in their jaws and use their jaws to crush the body of the animal that they have caught. The prey is usually drowned because the alligator or crocodile dives underwater with its catch.

This Nile crocodile has caught a gazelle.

Turn to page 103 to find the sticker that completes this scene.

CROCODILE FACT

Each year, crocodiles gather in the Mara River in Africa, waiting to catch the gnus that cross it on their journey to find fresh grass.

Digestion

Alligators and crocodiles swallow their prey whole or break it up into large pieces. They do not have to eat every day because their bodies use up energy slowly. This means they can survive for several months without food, especially in cooler weather, when they are not so active.

Keeping cool

Reptiles are ectothermic animals, which means that their body temperature is similar to that of their surroundings. Alligators and crocodiles are active only when their bodies are warm, so in the morning they lie out in the sun to warm up. During the hottest hours of the day, they either move into the shade or slip into the water to cool down.

Overheating

After a period of activity, such as running after prey, the alligator or crocodile's body temperature rises and it often overheats. When this happens, it has to cool down by resting in the shade or lying in the water.

Alligators and crocodiles open their mouths to help cool themselves down. This is called gaping.

Crocodiles and alligators lie in the shade during the hottest parts of the day.

CROCODILE FACT

When Nile crocodiles bask with their mouths open, birds called Egyptian plovers hop into their mouths and clean the crocodiles' teeth!

Find the sticker on page 105 that represents the correct answer.

QUESTION

True or false? Crocodiles have good underwater vision.

87

Living together

Alligators and crocodiles often meet up with other individuals of the same species to form groups. They bask in the sun together each day or gather at certain water holes. These groups are mostly females with one or two males. The individuals in these groups can recognize each other by the sounds they make.

Aggressive males

Male crocodiles and alligators don't like having many other males around, so larger and older males tend to chase away the smaller males. As a result, younger males usually hang around the outside of a group. During the breeding season, the large males guard their territories and they do not let any other males approach the females in their territory.

Turn to page 103 to find the sticker that completes this scene.

CROCODILE FACT

Scientists can tell the age of a crocodile by looking at growth rings on its scales.

This group of female alligators is basking in the sun. When they get too hot, they slip into the water.

Communication

Alligators and crocodiles make a wide range of sounds, including grunts, coughs, growls, and bellows. They make a long, loud hiss as a warning before they are going to attack.

Some alligators and crocodiles slap their heads against the water to make a sound that travels a long way, while the gharial makes a popping sound. Many species produce bubbles when they are underwater, and this creates sounds that others can hear.

This Nile crocodile inflates the pouch under its throat to make sounds.

ALLIGATOR AND CROCODILE FACT

Glands under the chin of an alligator or crocodile release a special scent that they use to recognize each other.

The vibrations are so strong, they make the water "dance" up and down.

Bellowing alligators

Male alligators **bellow** to attract a female and to warn off other males. When a male wants to bellow, he raises his head and tail out of the water, waves his tail back and forth, puffs out his throat, and shuts his mouth. Then he vibrates the air in his throat. This creates a vibration in the surrounding water that also causes the ground and any other objects in or near the water to vibrate.

Find the sticker on page 105 that represents the correct answer.

QUESTION
True or false?
Alligators swallow their prey whole or break it into large pieces.

Answer: True (see page 85)

Under threat

Alligators and crocodiles are hunted for their skin, which is used to make expensive shoes and handbags. In some places, so many alligators and crocodiles have been hunted that their numbers have fallen to very low levels.

Conservation successes

In 1971, the Australian saltwater crocodile had been hunted almost to extinction. Laws were passed to protect the crocodile, and now its numbers have returned to the levels that existed before hunting started. The numbers of crocodiles in Africa, South America, and North America are increasing, too, due to greater control of hunting.

Farming

Alligator and crocodile farms help protect alligators and crocodiles living in the wild. This is because the farmed animals provide skins and meat, leaving no reason to hunt wild animals.

Find the sticker on page 105 that represents the correct answer.

QUESTION

True or false? Growth rings on a crocodile's scales help scientists determine its age.

In some places, crocodiles and alligators are killed for their meat.

ALLIGATOR FACT

Before hunting was controlled in 1970, an estimated 10 million American alligators were killed for their skins.

Life cycle

The female Nile crocodile is ready to breed when she is about 10 years old. She lays between 30 and 80 eggs in a nest, and they hatch two to three months later. She cares for her young for up to two years. The Nile crocodile lives to be about 40 to 45 years old in the wild, but up to 80 years in captivity.

Hatchling

Full-grown crocodile

Juvenile

GLOSSARY

ancient very old

bask to lie out in the sun

bellow a roaring sound

camouflage coloring that blends in with the background

clutch a bunch of eggs laid at the same time by a female animal

ectothermic having a body temperature that is similar to that of the surrounding environment

extinct no longer in existence; a species that has died out completely

habitat the place in which an animal or plant lives

hatchling a young turtle or tortoise that has just emerged from the egg

hibernate to go into a type of deep sleep during the cold winter months

mangrove a group of tropical evergreen trees that grow closely together in the salty water along a coastline

migration a long journey made regularly by animals of the same species

milking the process of collecting snake venom

molt to shed skin, feathers, or hair

poison a harmful substance that prevents the body from working properly

predator an animal that hunts other animals

prey an animal that is hunted by a predator

GLOSSARY

pupil the dark spot in the middle of the eye

reptile an animal that is covered in hard scales and lays leathery eggs

scale a hard flake that is attached to the skin of a reptile or fish

sensor something that detects a stimulus, such as a touch, a vibration, or a smell

solitary living alone

species a group of animals that look alike and can breed together to produce young

terrapin a Native American word often used to describe small freshwater turtles

transparent clear; see-through

tropical the parts of the world near the equator that are hot year-round

venom poison produced by many snakes to kill their prey and to protect themselves

vibration a small back-and-forth movement

Create-a-scene stickers

97

Create-a-scene stickers

99

Create-a-scene stickers

Complete-the-scene stickers

Use the stickers on this page
to complete the scenes
throughout the book.

Page 29

Page 17

Page 57

Page 37

Page 44

Page 44

Page 12

Page 7

Page 28

Page 73

Page 88

Page 47

Page 84

Page 60

Answer stickers

Use the stickers on this page to complete the questions throughout the book.

Bonus stickers

Bonus stickers

Bonus stickers

113

Question

What's the Difference...

between an alligator and a crocodile?

Turn card over for answer.

Question

How do you know whether an alligator hatchling will be male or female?

Turn card over for answer.

Question

What's the Difference...

between a turtle and a tortoise?

Turn card over for answer.

Map It

Turtles and Tortoises

Which is the only continent where turtles and tortoises are NOT found?

Turn card over for answer.

Question

Animal Anatomy

How many teeth do turtles and tortoises have?

Turn card over for answer.

Match It Up

Match the question with the correct answer.

A. How many teeth does an alligator have?
B. How many pounds does a crocodile weigh?
C. How many hours can a crocodile remain underwater?
D. How many years do alligators live?

1. Up to 5
2. About 50
3. Up to 1,100
4. 74–80

Turn card over for answers.

Answer

Turtles have flatter shells; tortoises have dome-shaped shells. Also, because turtles spend a lot of time in the water, they have webbed feet. Land-dwelling tortoises do not have webbed feet.

Answer

Most of the hatchlings in an alligator nest will be male if the temperature stays between 89.6°F and 91.4°F. Most of the hatchlings will be female if the temperature is below 87.8°F or above 95°F.

Answer

Alligators have rounded snouts. When an alligator's mouth is closed, a socket in the upper jaw conceals the large fourth tooth in its lower jaw. Crocodiles have pointed, V-shaped snouts. A crocodile's fourth tooth is visible when its mouth is closed.

Answer

A. 4
B. 3
C. 1
D. 2

(Alligators in the wild live to be anywhere between 35–50 years old, but alligators in captivity can live up to 80 years!)

Answer

None! Turtles and tortoises chew food with a beaklike structure inside their powerful jaws.

Answer

Antarctica is the only continent without turtles and tortoises. Most turtles live in tropical or subtropical areas around the world.

There are almost
3,000 species
of snakes.

Turn card over for answer.

Crocodiles
can digest
most of what
they eat,
even bones.

Turn card over for answer.

Some large
snakes can
survive on one
meal for a
whole year.

Turn card over for answer.

True or False?

Turtles and
tortoises live
to be about
15 years old.

Turn card over for answer.

Question

Multiple Choice

Which of the following
reptiles stays to care
for its young after
laying eggs?

A. Snakes
B. Alligators
   and crocodiles
C. Turtles
   and tortoises

Turn card over for answer.

Match It Up

Match the animal with
its corresponding
description.

A. Turtle
B. Tortoise
C. Terrapin

1. Spends most of its time
   on land.
2. Is usually found in
   freshwater rather than
   salt water.
3. The majority of its life
   is spent in or near water.

Turn card over for answers.

True!
Many snakes do not eat regular meals. Because a snake's skin is elastic, it can stretch to make room for a large meal.

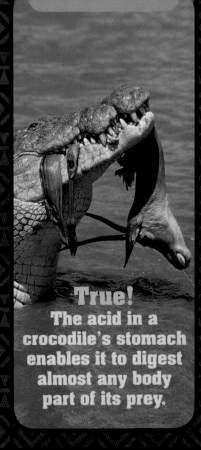

True!
The acid in a crocodile's stomach enables it to digest almost any body part of its prey.

True!
There are many different types of snakes, ranging from small garter snakes to gigantic boas and pythons.

Answer

A. 3

Turtles spend most of their lives in or by the sea, rivers, lakes, or swamps.

B. 1

Tortoises are land animals; some desert tortoises can survive without water for long stretches of time.

C. 2

Terrapin is the Native American word for "little turtle" and is often used to describe freshwater turtles.

Answer

B. Unlike most reptiles that leave after laying their eggs, female alligators and crocodiles guard their eggs from predators and usually stay with their hatchlings for several months.

Answer

False!
Turtles and tortoises have some of the longest life spans of any animal. In captivity, they can live to be about 70 years old. In the wild, they can live up to 50 years.

Ringing True

Q: How can a scientist tell how old a crocodile is?

A: Like trees, crocodiles have growth rings on their scales.

Having a Backbone

Did you know that a python's backbone is made up of 500 bones?

Need a Dentist?

Nile crocodiles get a free teeth cleaning by birds called Egyptian plovers when they bask in the sun with their mouths open.

Keeping Their Cool

After a period of activity, such as chasing prey, crocodiles and alligators tend to overheat. To cool down, they rest in the shade or lay in the water.

Word Scramble

M O R T C E H C E I T

Use the letters above to spell out a characteristic that causes reptiles to bask in the sun and cool off in the shade or in water.

Answer: Ectothermic

Tongue Talent

A snake can taste the air with its forked tongue. The tongue picks up scent particles in the air, and then inserts it into a special sense organ on the roof of its mouth.

Fun Fact

Protective Eye Gear
Crocodiles have three eyelids. The third eyelid is transparent and protects the eye in the water.

Fun Fact

What a Softy
A leatherback turtle does not have a hard shell like other turtles and tortoises. Its leathery skin and flexible body allow it to dive up to 3,000 feet below the ocean's surface and withstand water pressure that would crush a turtle with a harder shell.

Fun Fact

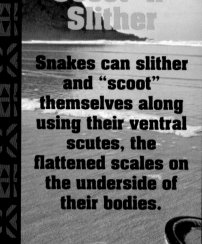

Scoot 'n' Slither
Snakes can slither and "scoot" themselves along using their ventral scutes, the flattened scales on the underside of their bodies.

Fun Fact

Making Sense
Crocodiles and alligators rely on tiny sensors around the face and mouth to help them locate prey. These sensors allow them to detect the vibrations and movements of other animals in the water.

Fun Facts

Turtles and Tortoises

Heaviest:
Leatherback turtle
(up to 1,800 pounds)

Lightest:
Speckled Cape tortoise
(up to 5 ounces)

Smallest:
Bog turtle (3–4.5 inches)

Fastest:
Leatherback turtle
(swims up to 22 miles per hour)

Joke

Q: What is a snake's favorite subject in school?

A: Hiss-tory!

Joke

Q: What do you get when you cross a newborn snake with a basketball?

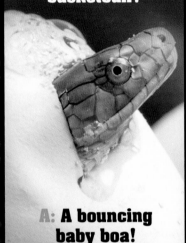

A: A bouncing baby boa!

Joke

Q: What do you give a sick alligator?

A: Gator-aid!

Fun Fact

Solar Power
Crocodiles have structures in their skin that trap heat to keep their cold-blooded bodies warm.

Fun Fact

Stink Bombs
Some turtles, like the snapping turtle and stinkpot, let off a smelly musk when they are disturbed.

Fun Fact

Seeing in Color
Turtles and tortoises have great eyesight and can see in color—even underwater.

Fun Fact

Good Vibrations
Turtles can feel vibrations in the water. This can help them locate food or steer clear of predators.